DURHAM CATHEDRAL

The Shrine of St Cuthbert

SCALA

Welcome

When you arrive in Durham one of the first things you see, whether arriving by train, road or foot, is Durham Cathedral. It stands out, towering above the skyline, sitting majestically alongside Durham Castle, with which it forms the Durham UNESCO World Heritage Site. The cathedral has you in awe and wonder at its immense design, the planning and effort needed to construct it. American writer Bill Bryson famously pronounced it as 'the best cathedral on planet earth'.

Durham Cathedral is steeped in history as well as being a living community. It is a place of Christian faith and spiritual enlightenment. We welcome over 750,000 visitors each year, who come from near and far. There are many reasons to visit: to marvel at the outstanding architecture; to pray on your own or to worship at a service; to journey as a pilgrim; to discover the stories of the northern saints; to enjoy amazing exhibitions and displays in the Museum, our world-class exhibition experience; to be inspired through our education programme for children, young people and adults; to attend a cultural event; or simply sit in silence and enjoy this holy site.

Whatever your reason for visiting, Durham Cathedral will always be with you. It is truly a beacon of the North, once experienced never forgotten.

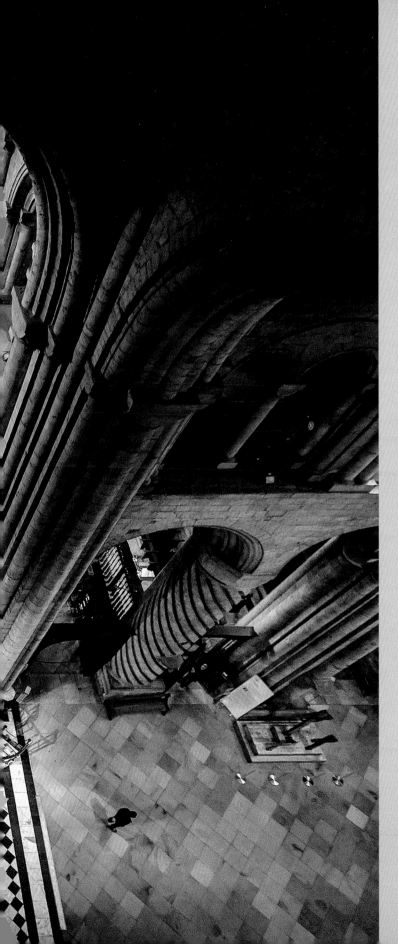

Contents

Introduction

Durham Cathedral is a Christian church of the Anglican Communion, the shrine of St Cuthbert, the seat of the bishop of Durham and a focus of pilgrimage and spirituality in North East England. Walking around Durham Cathedral, you are following in the steps of millions of pilgrims who have made their way to the shrine of St Cuthbert, and the resting place of the Venerable Bede.

The cathedral is also one of the great buildings of Europe. Set grandly on a rocky promontory next to Durham Castle, with the medieval city huddled below and the river sweeping around, the profile of this UNESCO World Heritage Site is instantly recognisable.

The cathedral's history begins not in Durham at all, however, but on the 'Holy Island' of Lindisfarne, 130km/80m to the north, off the Northumberland coast. In 995, St Cuthbert's relics were brought from Lindisfarne to Durham and the Anglo Saxons built a cathedral to house them. After the Norman Conquest, in 1083, a community of Benedictine monks was established on the peninsula, and it was they who built the present cathedral, in turn prompting the development of the medieval city and, much later, the founding of the university.

Started in 1093, the cathedral was a pioneering building – which makes the 40 or

Stunning light effects on the north face of the cathedral during the biannual Lumiere festival celebrating its rich history. Images from November 2013 showing 'Crown of Light' by Ross Ashton, Robert Ziegler and John Del'Nero

so years it took to complete an astonishing achievement. Its founder, Bishop William of St Calais (or Carileph), no doubt wanted to construct a building worthy of the great saint it housed and of the God he had so faithfully served.

The Normans also wished to make an unambiguous statement to both the defeated Saxons and to the Scots further north about where authority lay in these newly conquered lands. The cathedral was a fitting symbol of the power of the prince bishops, who were charged by the king to defend the realm from the constant threat of invasion. Perched on its rocky

peninsula next to a great Norman fortification, the cathedral therefore spoke of human as well as divine power. 'Half church of God, half castle 'gainst the Scot', said Sir Walter Scott, in the frequently quoted lines engraved on Prebends' Bridge (from where one of the finest views of Durham Cathedral can be enjoyed).

So the cathedral is a glorious paradox. It tells of the power of prelates and kings, but it also tells of the more enduring power of goodness, simplicity, holiness and devotion to God. It remains what it always was: a sign of God's presence in the world and the promise that his kingdom will come.

'Durham ... is one of the great architectural experiences of Europe.'

Sir Nikolaus Pevsner,
The Buildings of England: County Durham (1953)

Entering the Cathedral

The 'show' front of the cathedral is to the north, on the Palace Green side. The huge mass of the building (total length 14m/469ft) closes in the entire south side of Palace Green, balancing if not overshadowing the castle opposite.

The exterior marks out the different components of the cathedral: a Norman nave and quire with transepts between; beyond the quire a thirteenth-century Gothic extension, the Chapel of the Nine Altars; and beyond the western towers a late Norman extension, the twelfth-century Galilee Chapel.

The western towers, built above the precipitous gorge of the river, date from the twelfth and thirteenth centuries. The great central tower (66m/218ft in height) was the last major addition to the fabric, displaying fine late-fifteenth-century perpendicular Gothic detail.

The sanctuary knocker on the main door is a replica of the famous twelfth-century original.

Until 1623, when the right of sanctuary was abolished, those being pursued for certain crimes could enter the cathedral by grasping hold of the ring and be offered a safe place or 'sanctuary' for 37 days. After that they would be required to leave the country or face trial.

CLOCKWISE FROM ABOVE: The cathedral from Palace Green; the rose window at the east end; the sanctuary knocker; the legend of the dun cow

Nave

The nave (Latin *navis*, 'ship', reflecting the idea that the nave of a church is like an upturned ship) is the body of the church, where people are free to enter and where large cathedral services take place to this day. Try to imagine it without seating, for this was a space for crowds to attend services or walk in procession. Otherwise, the nave is much as it was nine centuries ago.

The great piers, marching eastwards on either side in an alternating rhythm, convey an impression of vastness and antiquity. They reinforce the sense that the cathedral is a sequence of thresholds leading the eye and the pilgrim from one room to the next, a journey that culminates at the high altar and the rose window above. The compound piers mark the division of the nave into rectangular bays, with their columns soaring upwards to the stone vault. The round drum piers with their carved geometric patterns are a sculptural *tour de force*, possibly a Durham innovation. Their eye-catching designs of chevrons, vertical fluting and lozenges are matched in pairs across the nave. This counterpoint between large-scale effect and small-scale attention to detail is carried through the entire building – in the chevron decoration that adorns many of the arches and vault ribs, in the pier capitals and in the intersecting patterns of the blind arcading on the walls of the aisles.

The proportions of the nave are carefully contrived to balance the two effects the builders wished to create. To emphasise the great length of the church, they adopted the standard three-storey elevation common in Norman churches; the nave arcade itself (the series of round-headed arches on each side), the triforium above, and the clerestory at the top. Highlighted by the lines of the string courses above and beneath the gallery, these strongly emphasise the horizontal aspect of the building. Counterbalancing this is the equally powerful vertical thrust provided by the piers,

RIGHT: Looking up the nave to the rose window at the east end

especially the compound piers that run directly from floor to vault and intersect with the horizontals. The mathematics of these proportions is no accident. The circumference of the piers is exactly the same as their height, and explains why the nave is so satisfying a space. It is both light enough to lift the eye and the spirit, and substantial enough to connect the parts to the whole and anchor it to the earth on which it stands.

The nave reveals the ground-breaking character of this extraordinary building; here at Durham, for the first time in England, the masons solved the engineering problem of how to throw a stone vault safely across such a large space. The nave vault is entirely Norman work,

completed in 1133. But the arches that spring from the great compound piers on either side to span the width of the nave are pointed, rather than the round-headed type associated with Norman architecture, as seen in the arcades, the gallery and the clerestory. The pointed arch is a much more efficient load-bearing structure than the round-headed arch. Together with the diagonal ribs that criss-cross the vault, this enabled the nave to be constructed entirely of stone. To roof a width of 10m (32ft) with a vault rising to 23m (75ft) was a pioneering achievement that paved the way for the emergence of the Gothic style in the next century.

The most important piece of furniture in the nave is the font, close to the main entrance. This is

the place of Christian initiation, where children and adults are admitted into membership of the church through baptism. Traditionally, the font is placed near the west door of the church as a symbol of entrance and belonging, mirroring the other principal focal point of the church, the high altar at the east end. So the entire length of the church is poised between the font, as the place of beginnings, and the altar as the place of climax and consummation. The nave is a symbol of the journey of religious faith and human experience.

Specifically, the font stands for the central affirmations of Christian faith, summed up in the creed that is recited at every baptism. The large gathering space around it allows a congregation

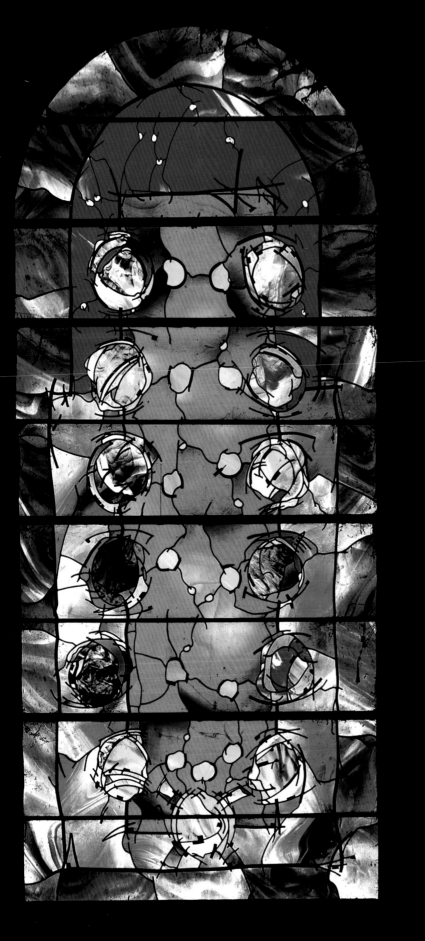

SAINT · CUTHBERT · BISHOP · OF · LINDISFARNE

SAINT · OSWALD · KING · OF · NORTHUMBRIA

PATRICK · ALINGTON
JUVENIS · SUIS · CARISSIMUS
DEO · SINABUS · CARIOR
IN · ITALIA · MILITANS · DECESSIT
AD · MCMXLIII

to witness the baptism liturgy, but also signals that the nave is a place where the baptised people of God gather together for worship. The marble bowl for the water of baptism dates from 1663. The magnificent font cover is of the same period, a fine example of the luscious woodwork throughout the building dating from the time of the seventeenth-century bishop of Durham, John Cosin. It is 12m (40ft) high, one of the tallest in the land and is intended to signify the link between earth and heaven in baptism.

The organ case near the south door dates from a little later in the seventeenth century and originally stood over the quire screen. The Miners' Memorial east of the door also includes woodwork from this screen. It was created in 1947 as a symbol of Durham Cathedral's long association with the mining industry and as a reminder of its human cost.

Burials were discouraged in a building overshadowed by the presence of Cuthbert's burial place, so there are few monuments in the nave. This creates an impression of uncluttered simplicity and restraint within architecture of such nobility. The south arcade holds a few memorials, the most impressive of these being the tomb-chest of 1388 of John, Lord Neville, a wealthy benefactor of the cathedral priory.

Nearby is the mutilated monument of his father Ralph, the first layman to be given the honour of a cathedral burial for his victorious part in the Battle of Neville's Cross in 1346. Opposite is a memorial dated 1839 to a local headmaster, James Britton, whose relaxed posture makes an interesting contrast to the formality of the architecture.

The stonework of Prior Fossor's great fourteenth-century west window shows how well the mature Gothic style harmonises with the Romanesque. Its coloured glass, as with many of the windows, is Victorian. At the west end of the aisles are twentieth-century windows depicting St Cuthbert and King Oswald of Northumbria, whose head is buried with Cuthbert's remains. The colourful 'Daily Bread' window near the north door is an abstract interpretation of the Last Supper at which Jesus broke bread with his disciples before his death.

At the head of the nave is the crossing under the central tower. Here there would once have been a screen separating the people's nave from the quire reserved for the daily worship of the monastic community. At the far end is a glimpse of the sanctuary and, within it, the high altar. Behind this, not visible from the nave, is the shrine of St Cuthbert.

OPPOSITE: Stained glass in the nave: the modern 'Daily Bread' window designed by Mark Angus (FAR LEFT), and two twentieth-century windows designed by Hugh Easton showing St Cuthbert (NEAR LEFT TOP) and St Oswald

ABOVE: Nineteenth-century memorial to local headmaster James Britton

South Transept and Durham Light Infantry Chapel

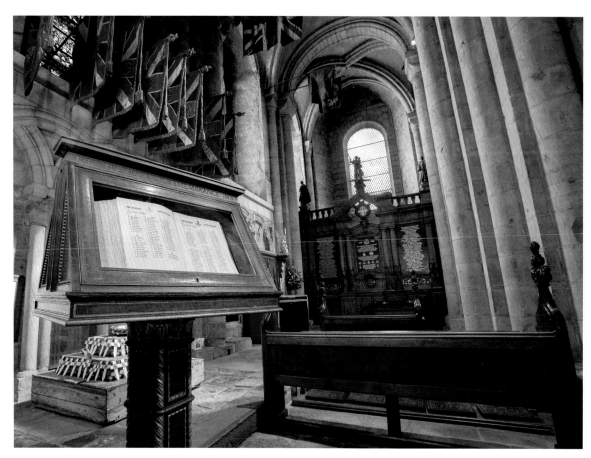

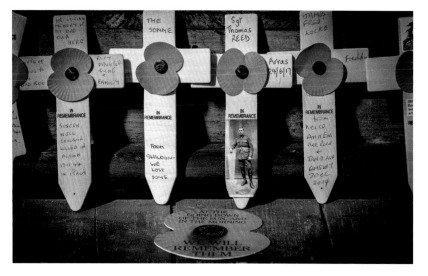

Medieval churches were usually built on a west-east axis, so that worshippers faced not only the high altar but also the rising sun and the holy city of Jerusalem, symbols of the resurrection of Christ and of the heavenly city promised to the faithful. Like many churches, the original Norman cathedral had a 'footprint' shaped like a Latin cross, to which later additions were made. The arms of the cross are known as transepts, extensions to the building on the north and south sides.

The south transept contains one of the cathedral's most famous curiosities, the highly coloured medieval clock. It is believed this was originally constructed by Prior Castell in the late fifteenth or early sixteenth century but was

altered in the seventeenth. It was taken down in 1845, as it was thought by the Victorians to be too frivolous for a serious building like a cathedral. Its reconstruction as a working clock in 1938 was the first of many projects funded by the Friends of Durham Cathedral, which was formed in 1933.

The chapel in the transept was furnished in 1924 as a memorial to the Durham Light Infantry, whose honours are recorded here alongside books of remembrance. On the west wall opposite hangs a miners' banner, another link with the working traditions of North East England. Below it is a memorial to Bishop Shute Barrington (died 1826), a fine piece of sculpture in white marble by the renowned Sheffield sculptor Francis Chantrey.

CLOCKWISE FROM FAR LEFT:
Individual memorial crosses in the chapel; a book of remembrance standing open below the regimental colours; the medieval clock; miners' banner hanging in the south transept

Tower and Crossing

At the crossing, the east-west and north-south axes of the church meet, a point of rest around which the principal spaces of the Norman church are organised. The view westwards down the nave is especially beautiful, particularly when the setting sun lights up the great west window, as is the view east to the rose window in the early morning. The transepts to north and south balance the length of the church, while eastwards the crossing marks a clear threshold as the gateway to the quire.

To look upwards is to appreciate for the first time the height of the lantern, the interior of the fifteenth-century tower; the crown of the tower vault is 47 m (155 ft) high and above this are the ringing chamber and belfry. The climb to the top of the tower is a long one, over 325 steps, but is worth the effort, offering wonderful views of the Durham World Heritage Site, the city of Durham, the wooded loop of the River Wear and further afield across the surrounding countryside.

The furnishings in the crossing form a Gothic-revival group by the Victorian architect George Gilbert Scott. His three-arched screen of 1876 stands on the site of the medieval pulpitum, a stone screen that once enclosed the monastic quire. Its successor, Cosin's seventeenth-century organ screen, was removed in the early nineteenth century to open up an uninterrupted vista towards the high altar.

CLOCKWISE FROM LEFT: The nave, north transept and crossing from above; looking up the tower to the lantern; the quire and high altar seen through George Gilbert Scott's crossing screen

19

Quire

The quire, and beyond it the sanctuary, were the heart of the monastic church. Here, in a space once entirely enclosed by a stone screen (the pulpitum), the monks of the cathedral priory would gather seven times each day to sing the divine office. This offering of daily praise and prayer was known as the *Opus Dei* or 'the work of God'. Around it the whole of monastic life was organised.

In 1539 the monastery was dissolved by order of Henry VIII, one of the last foundations to be suppressed in England, and in 1541 it was re-founded as an Anglican cathedral. The cycle of daily worship continued in the Reformed style familiar to us now as the services of Morning and Evening Prayer in the *Book of Common Prayer* of the Church of England. Apart from the Commonwealth period (1649–1660), when the cathedral was closed for worship on the order of Oliver Cromwell, this rhythm has continued each day ever since. The Cathedral Choir now sings Evensong six days a week during term-time, together with Sunday morning Matins and sung Eucharist, the principal service of the week.

As was usual in medieval church buildings, the cathedral was constructed from east to west, so that the high altar and the shrine of St Cuthbert could be installed as soon as possible and worship and pilgrimage begun. The east end of the church down to the crossing was complete by 1104, although the current quire vault dates only from the thirteenth century, following the failure of the original Norman vault.

The appearance of the quire at ground level, however, is now more of the seventeenth than the twelfth century, dominated as it is by the elaborate carved woodwork of Bishop Cosin's stalls. These were made in 1665, not long after the cathedral had been restored as a place of worship at the end of the Commonwealth. Their tall 'Gothic' canopies seem to have been inspired by the medieval stone screen behind the altar, but interpreted in a way that belongs

CLOCKWISE FROM BELOW: Decorative bench-end in the quire stalls; carved misericord; looking up the quire to the high altar

LAUDATE DOMIN

Richly decorated organ-pipes (LEFT);
a cherub's head at the base of a
canopy in the quire stalls (RIGHT)

entirely to the Renaissance. The skilled craftsmen who worked on them also created furnishings for several parish churches in County Durham. The Latin inscriptions are inspired by the Old Testament; their theme is the praise of God through music and are translated as:

> *Play (the harp) boys wisely*
> *praise the Lord in the drum and choir*
> *let us praise famous men*
> *men having zeal and beauty*
> *praise the Lord in strings and organ*
> *play (the harp) boys wisely.*

The seats of the canons' stalls (as they originally were) in the back row have beautifully carved misericords beneath. The quire pulpit carries a hanging designed by Leonard Childs and executed by the Cathedral Broderers, a team of volunteer embroiderers who create and maintain the cathedral's vestments and other sewn items. It depicts the traditional symbols of the four evangelists: the man of St Matthew, the lion of St Mark, the ox of St Luke and the eagle of St John.

The organ was originally built by 'Father' Henry Willis in 1876, so-called in honour of his expertise. This replaced the famous Father Smith organ of 1686 that had stood over the quire screen (some of the old organ case survives near the west end). In 1905 the Willis instrument was rebuilt by the Durham firm of organ builders Harrison and Harrison, who continue to care for it today. A four-manual

instrument, it is reckoned to be one of the finest organs of the Romantic era in England.

Beyond the stalls on the south side stands the bishop's throne. A cathedral is so called because it houses the bishop's seat or *cathedra*, symbolising his or her ministry of teaching, pastoral care and evangelism in the diocese. This extraordinary highly-decorated piece was designed by Bishop Hatfield (died 1381) as both his throne and his tomb. His episcopate was perhaps the height of the Durham palatinate, in which prince bishops exercised not only spiritual but political jurisdiction, with powers to mint coinage, raise an army and hear cases at law. Only in the early nineteenth century were these 'temporal' powers finally absorbed by the Crown.

Sanctuary

East of the quire lies the sanctuary. It houses the high altar, which is the principal focus of the church. Here the sacrament of the Eucharist (the Mass or Holy Communion) is celebrated, the bread and wine representing Christ's body and blood given for the world. It is the place of recognition and reception, where the journey begun at the font reaches its culmination.

The sanctuary is marked out as a point of climax by the great stone reredos behind the altar. This, the Neville screen, is one of the treasures of Durham Cathedral. It was largely the gift of John, Lord Neville, whose tomb-chest is in the nave. Completed in 1380 out of stone thought to come from Caen in northern France, it would originally have been brightly painted, and statues of angels and saints would have stood in each of the 107 niches.

All this was swept away in the years that followed the Reformation. The alabaster figures

were, it is said, buried by the monks before they could be destroyed; if so, their whereabouts remains one of the great mysteries of Durham. The screen is still impressive today for the purity of its stone and the simplicity of its Gothic lines. On either side of the altar, incorporated into the screen, are the sedilia, stone seats for those assisting at services at the high altar.

The high altar itself is modern, but within it stands a modest seventeenth-century marble altar which is used during Holy Week, the annual celebration of the death and resurrection of Jesus. The coloured and patterned marble pavement in the quire and sanctuary is again the work of Scott, of a piece with his pulpit and screen at the crossing.

CLOCKWISE FROM FAR LEFT: The high altar and the Neville screen; Scott's marble sanctuary floor; two aumbries, or sacred cupboards

South Quire Aisle

The south quire aisle leads to Cuthbert's shrine, up the stone steps to the left. High up on a pier outside the shrine is the banner of St Cuthbert, a contemporary replica based on the description of the medieval original that once hung in this part of the cathedral and which was carried into battle from time to time to secure English victory against the Scots.

Opposite, and best viewed from the steps, is the glowing 'Transfiguration' window. This was designed by Tom Denny and installed in 2010 in memory of Michael Ramsey (1904–88), once a canon and then bishop of Durham, before becoming archbishop first of York and then of Canterbury. The Transfiguration of Jesus was one of Ramsey's favourite themes; Jesus is glorified and acknowledged as the Son of God in the presence of chosen disciples and of the heavenly witnesses Moses and Elijah.

The south quire aisle also contains a coloured twentieth-century window depicting North East England, which was given in 1995 to commemorate the millennium of the first cathedral's foundation.

CLOCKWISE FROM FAR LEFT: Detail of the 'Transfiguration' window gifted by the Friends of Durham Cathedral; steps leading to the shrine of St Cuthbert, with the modern St Cuthbert banner (an authentic reconstruction of a medieval banner that was lost before the Reformation, this was made and embroidered by Ruth O'Leary, bringing together components created by other artisans, and is regularly used in procession); general view of the 'Transfiguration' window; another detail; window celebrating the cathedral's millennium, designed by Joseph Nuttgens, using Sunderland glass installed by glazier Bernard Seaton

Shrine of St Cuthbert

The shrine of St Cuthbert is the emotional and spiritual climax of the building. The saint is buried beneath a simple stone slab that bears his name in Latin: CVTHBERTVS. Nearby is a mutilated fifteenth-century statue of Cuthbert holding the head of the Northumbrian King Oswald, which is also buried in the grave. Above is a twentieth-century canopy by Ninian Comper depicting Christ in Glory. On either side are contemporary banners by Thetis Blacker of Cuthbert and Oswald. Candles and kneelers invite contemplation at the shrine of one of England's most remarkable men.

Cuthbert, a Northumbrian, was born in about 634 and in his youth guarded sheep in the Scottish border hill country. One night he saw a light descend from the night sky and then return; believing it to be a human soul, he took it as a sign to enter the monastery at Melrose. The date, 31 August 651, also marked the death of the Irish monk Aidan, who had established a monastery on the 'holy island' of Lindisfarne in his mission to reconvert Northumbria to Christianity at the invitation of King Oswald (c.605–42). Cuthbert later moved to Lindisfarne, first as prior to the community there, then as bishop.

Cuthbert's holiness, learning and love of nature, his care for people and the fervour of his preaching were already legendary in his lifetime. When his body was disinterred 11 years after his death, it was found to be miraculously undecayed and a shrine was set up to honour him. This was Northumbria's artistic golden age, its cultural and intellectual achievements reflected in the Lindisfarne Gospels, written on the island early in the eighth century 'in honour of God and St Cuthbert'.

By the ninth century, Viking raids drove the 'community of St Cuthbert', carrying with them the relics of Cuthbert and the Lindisfarne Gospels, to seek a more secure home. After a long journey around the north of England, they finally arrived

CLOCKWISE FROM LEFT: Cuthbert statue; Cuthbert banner; the simple marble burial slab; Oswald banner

in Durham in 995. As they approached the peninsula, legend has it that the cart bearing the coffin stuck fast in the ground and a monk dreamed they should go to a place called Dun Holm. When they heard the locals talk about a lost cow which would be found at Dun Holm, they took it as a sign from Cuthbert. The wheels of the cart then moved and the coffin was duly brought on to the peninsula, where it has remained ever since.

The community's first church on the site lasted less than 100 years. In May 1083 a Benedictine convent was founded in place of the existing religious house, and a decade later the Norman cathedral was begun as a more splendid home for the shrine. Cuthbert's relics were installed in their present position in 1104. Durham rapidly became the foremost pilgrimage destination in England, and one of the wealthiest. Only with the martyrdom of Thomas Becket in 1170 did Canterbury eclipse it, although Durham's energetic promotion of pilgrimage ensured that the shrine continued to attract pilgrims throughout the Middle Ages.

In late 1537 the king's commissioners came to Durham to dismantle the shrine. It was stripped of its gold, silver and jewels and levelled to the ground. When Cuthbert's coffin was uncovered, they found not dust and bones but a body in priestly vestments 'fresh, safe and not consumed'. It was therefore left alone and re-interred. The grave has twice been opened up since then, in 1827 and 1899. The stark black slab that bears his name is, perhaps, as eloquent a tribute to the simple prior, bishop and hermit of Lindisfarne as his elaborately jewelled shrine had once been.

In 2005 St Cuthbert's name was reinstated in the legal dedication of the cathedral, from which it had been removed in the sixteenth century. It is now dedicated to 'Christ, Blessed Mary the Virgin and St Cuthbert'.

Some of the precious artefacts from Cuthbert's tomb that were removed in 1827, collectively known as the Treasures of St Cuthbert, are on display in the fourteenth-century Great Kitchen, which forms part of the cathedral's museum exhibition experience.

St Cuthbert's shrine,
with the canopy above
showing Christ in glory

Chapel of the Nine Altars

At the east end, the cathedral opens up unexpectedly. A line on the floor of the feretory, the shrine chapel, indicates the curved apse with which the east end originally ended. As the numbers of pilgrims grew, it became necessary to enlarge the space around Cuthbert's shrine to accommodate them, and the Chapel of the Nine Altars was built between 1242 and 1280. The chapel is as pure a piece of Early English Gothic architecture as the nave is Norman. The 'join' happens in the easternmost bay of the quire, though the entire quire vault also dates from this period. The resemblance to the Early English cathedral at Salisbury is no accident, as Bishop le Poore of Salisbury instigated the work after becoming Bishop of Durham. The layout of the chapel, spreading out into eastern transepts, was modelled on Fountains Abbey in Yorkshire. The vertical thrust is emphasised by the lower floor level, by the tall lancet windows and by the slender shafts of local County Durham Frosterley marble running from floor to vault. This vault gave the masons some trouble, for on the south side the ribs 'miss' a central roof boss.

The rose window is a late-eighteenth-century reworking of a medieval predecessor. The beautiful 'Joseph' window on the north end has double tracery straddling the wall passage in between. The nine altars originally stood against the east wall, enabling all the priest members of the monastery to celebrate Mass daily at different altars. The central altar of St Aidan has hangings made by the Cathedral Broderers depicting the northern saints. The altars to St Hild (left) and St Margaret of Scotland (right) commemorate female saints associated with North East England. The hangings on the Margaret altar were completed by the Cathedral Broderers in 2005. The painting near the St Margaret altar is by Paula Rego; commissioned by the cathedral and dedicated in 2004, it shows the saint near the end of her life, together with her son David, future king of Scotland and himself one of Scotland's best-loved saints.

On the floor by the altar is a plaque commemorating the Scottish prisoners incarcerated in the cathedral by Oliver Cromwell after the battle of Dunbar in 1650, during a severe winter. It is not known how many died through hunger, sickness or cold. The contemporary sculptures nearby are the work of local Durham sculptor Fenwick Lawson. Particularly impressive is his *Pietà*, depicting the sorrowful mother of Jesus after the crucifixion, with the body of her dead son taken down from the cross.

At the north end of the Chapel of the Nine Altars a marble statue commemorates Bishop van Mildert, the last of the prince bishops who, with the Cathedral Chapter, founded Durham University in 1832. Other bishops and deans are commemorated on ledger stones in the floor.

ABOVE: The eighteenth-century rose window

OPPOSITE: *Pietà*, by local sculptor Fenwick Lawson (FAR LEFT); portrait of St Margaret and her son David, by Paula Rego (ABOVE); statue of Bishop van Mildert (BELOW)

CLOCKWISE FROM RIGHT: Detail from the Lesotho banner, showing village life; a Bedesman seated on the Bedesmen's bench; *Lama Sabachthani* by Kirill Sokolov

North Quire Aisle and North Transept

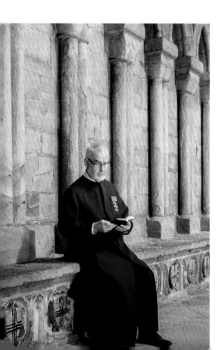

The quire aisles lead from the Chapel of the Nine Altars to the transepts. In the wall of the north aisle are the Bedesmen's benches (from the Old English *bede*, meaning a prayer). These church officers are lay people who have for centuries played a key role in the daily life of the cathedral, not least in its worship. Opposite is a monument to a great Victorian bishop, Joseph Lightfoot (died 1889), one of the most learned theologians of his day.

Like the south, the north transept has a chapel behind its pillars – the Gregory Chapel – formerly the Benedict Chapel. In the medieval period the transept had three chapels; the Gregory, the Benedict and the jointly named

St Nicholas and St Giles. The Gregory Chapel, of today, was refurbished in the twentieth century for personal prayer, and the sacrament is reserved there. The Benedict Altar, on a moveable platform against the north wall of the transept, is used in the crossing for Sunday worship. It is dedicated to St Benedict, whose rule for monks was followed in the Middle Ages in Durham and thousands of other Benedictine monastic houses across Europe, and continues to be observed in monasteries to this day. A banner on the wall marks the link between the dioceses of Durham and Lesotho in southern Africa. The curious white marble monument just inside the quire aisle is to Matthew Woodifield (died 1826).

CLOCKWISE FROM LEFT: St Gregory window, designed by Hugh Eastman; private prayer in the Gregory chapel; nineteenth-century monument of Matthew Woodfield, a headteacher of Durham School

Galilee Chapel and the Venerable Bede

Walking west down the nave entails crossing a line in black marble on the floor near the font. This marked a boundary which women were forbidden to cross, for this church belonged to an all-male Benedictine community. An early attempt to build a Lady Chapel for women east of the shrine was aborted, owing to the instability of the foundations. In 1170 Bishop Hugh le Puiset (sometimes known as Pudsey) began to construct a Lady Chapel at the opposite end of the cathedral. This is the Galilee Chapel, one of the most exquisite parts of the building, entered through doors in the west wall.

The Galilee is partly a chapel, partly a porch or narthex; a place to assemble before and after services. Such porches are common in Romanesque churches in France, such as Vézelay. Galilee was the homeland of Jesus from where he 'went up' to Jerusalem, so the Galilee Chapel was a place of arrival from which to go to the main cathedral. Galilee is also where the risen Jesus promised to meet his disciples, having gone ahead of them. So the Galilee Chapel was also a place of departure and dismissal, and great cathedral services and processions would often have ended here.

The Galilee Chapel is still Norman in style, with its four arcades of round arches decorated with elaborate chevrons, but it is much lighter in

LEFT: Elaborate chevrons on the Norman arcading, with the tomb of the Venerable Bede on the right

ABOVE: Inscription on the tomb of the Venerable Bede in the chapel

RIGHT: Detail of the wooden statue of Mary by Polish sculptor Joseph Pyrz

feel than the nave, and its air of luminous transparency suggests that the Gothic era is not far away. Some see in the architecture of this chapel an echo of the great mosque at Córdoba in Spain. The original great west doorway into the cathedral can be seen here, blocked since the fifteenth century by the great altar and tomb-chest of Thomas Langley (died 1437), cardinal and twice chancellor of England. The painting of the crucifixion has been attributed to the sixteenth-century Flemish painter van Orley.

On the north side of the chapel are a number of medieval wall paintings, rare survivors which give some idea of what the cathedral would have looked like before the Reformation. On the wall behind the modern altar are a bishop and a king, almost certainly St Cuthbert and St Oswald, and dating from around the time of the Galilee's construction in the twelfth century. Above the arcade is a later series of paintings from the thirteenth or fourteenth centuries, showing the crucifixion

of Christ, and the apostles as martyrs dying for their faith. Fragments of fourteenth- and fifteenth-century stained glass from all over the cathedral are preserved in the windows.

Like the feretory or shrine chapel, the Galilee holds a firm place in the affection of people across North East England for the shrine it contains. A simple Latin inscription on a tomb-chest identifies its contents as the bones of the Venerable Bede. It is thanks to Bede's writings that we know so much about the church in England in Anglo-Saxon times, and in particular about St Cuthbert. Known as the 'Father of English History', Bede was born in about 673, and joined the monastic community at Wearmouth aged seven, transferring to the newly founded monastery of Jarrow soon afterwards, where he spent the rest of his life. He was the most accomplished scholar of his day – historian, theologian, poet, scientist, biographer, and author of many commentaries on the Bible. Like the Lindisfarne Gospels, his writings show the heights achieved

by the flowering of Northumbrian civilisation in the eighth century.

Bede died and was buried at Jarrow in 735. In about 1022 his relics were stolen (or removed for safe keeping) by a Durham monk and brought to the cathedral, where they were initially placed with Cuthbert's and later moved to a shrine of their own in the Galilee Chapel. This did not survive the dissolution; as with Cuthbert, the simplicity of Bede's modern tomb is an apt comment on the humility of his life. The recess behind has a quotation from Bede's commentary on the Apocalypse (or Book of Revelation)

praising 'Christ the Morning Star'. It was designed by Frank Roper and George Pace in 1971. The inscription is interpreted in the lamp above the tomb, designed by Christopher Downes and given by the North East of England Rotary Clubs (District 1030) in 2005.

The wooden statue of Mary, by the twentieth-century Polish sculptor Joseph Pyrz, identifies the Galilee as the Lady Chapel. The square 'Last Supper' table has a marquetry top that unfolds to reveal wooden sculptures of emblems of the Eucharist. It was made by the contemporary sculptor Colin Wilbourn.

For over 1000 years the treasure of the Christian gospel has been proclaimed in Durham, expressed in people's lives, in our history as a monastery and church, in words, music, art, study and service. In this exhibition, we open up that treasure and tell some of our Christian story through a world-class visitor experience, located at the heart of the most intact surviving set of medieval monastic buildings in the UK. Visitors embark on a journey of discovery through some of the cathedral's most spectacular spaces, including the Monks' Dormitory and the Great Kitchen, as the remarkable story of Durham Cathedral and its incredible collections is revealed.

The journey begins in the fourteenth-century Monks' Dormitory, with interactive exhibits and activities for visitors of all ages. An exhibition of Roman, Anglo-Saxon and Viking stones provides a dramatic opening, highlighting the role of North East England in the development of Christianity across the whole country. Sights, sounds and smells evoke life in a medieval monastery, while an interactive timeline charts the history of Durham Cathedral from the arrival of the Community of St Cuthbert in Durham to cathedral life today.

Visitors continue to the Collections Gallery, a state-of-the-art exhibition space with a rolling programme of displays showcasing items from the cathedral's internationally renowned collections, before reaching the spectacular Great Kitchen. This impressive space, with its octagonal-vaulted ceiling, is the permanent home of the Treasures of St Cuthbert, some of the world's most precious Anglo-Saxon artefacts.

The visitor experience draws to a close with the Pilgrimage Gallery and the Community Gallery, before returning to the medieval cloister, a fitting end to a journey through Durham's spectacular monastic architecture.

The making of the Museum

The exhibition spaces of the museum allow the cathedral to display precious objects from its internationally important collections, for which it previously lacked both space and specialist facilities. The galleries are designed to meet the highest environmental control standards.

Embarking on such an ambitious development project required significant planning and funding. The story began in 2012 with the creation of the new Cathedral Shop in the undercroft. This important first phase created space for the new exhibition route. Work started in July 2014, following a grant of £3.9m from the Heritage Lottery Fund and planning consent from the Cathedral's Fabric Commission for England. An additional £8m from trusts, foundations and the general public made the completion of this ambitious development project possible.

The transformation of the cathedral's monastic spaces presented many challenges, and relied on the talents of the cathedral's in-house team of stonemasons, joiners and electricians. In the Monks' Dormitory, huge walls had their joints meticulously chiselled out by stonemasons, to be replaced with a more sustainable lime-based mortar, while the cathedral's joiners painstakingly created 89 new doors for the bookcases. The design of the exhibition in the Monks' Dormitory was developed by specialist museum designers Studio MB.

For the Collections Gallery and Great Kitchen, bespoke cases were commissioned from specialist manufacturers to achieve the environmental and security conditions necessary for exhibiting sensitive artefacts from the cathedral's collections, as well as temporary, complementary loans from other world-class institutions. A comprehensive archaeological survey was carried out in the Great Kitchen and covey before restoration work could begin, which unveiled numerous archaeological remains, from oyster shells to Roman pottery.

Following the completion of the restoration and conservation work, interactive exhibits and activities were developed, alongside interpretation to bring the story of Durham Cathedral to life. With a rolling programme of exhibitions and state-of-the-art technology, the museum is the new must-see visitor attraction in Durham.

The Monks' Dormitory

The fourteenth-century Monks' Dormitory, above the west range of the cloister, provides a dramatic welcome. The long oak-beamed room is the only intact surviving monastic dormitory in England and one of the most spectacular English medieval halls. The cavernous space was once divided by wooden partitions into narrow cubicles, in which the cathedral's resident Benedictine monks would study and sleep. The day stair, which visitors now ascend as they enter the museum, was used by monks to access the cloister. The remains of the night stair, used by the monks to enter the cathedral for prayer during the night, are still visible behind the Welcome Desk.

Since the dissolution of the monastery in 1539, the Monks' Dormitory has been used for a variety of purposes, serving from 1856 as a library. The museum has transformed the Monks' Dormitory into an accessible, visitor-friendly exhibition space, while retaining and enhancing its function as a working library – reflecting the concept of living heritage which the museum. Durham has always been a place of scholarship. Study was an important part of the life of the medieval monks and an expression of their love of God and his world, and the Cathedral Library continues to play an integral role in the life of Durham Cathedral. The Monks' Dormitory houses the cathedral's modern theology collection, including the Archdeacon Sharp Library and the Chapter Library, and is accessible to all members of the local community including Durham University students. Located at the south end of the Monks' Dormitory, the library offers a reading space for academics and researchers.

Durham Cathedral possesses an important collection of around 30,000 early printed books, music and antiquary collections, housed in the recently restored Refectory Library. Although

not open to the general public on a daily basis, the Refectory Library is regularly used for talks and displays. This spectacular space was originally used as a dining room by the monks of Durham, and the fifteenth-century wooden benches still survive.

The cathedral also possesses one of the most important collections of medieval manuscripts of any English cathedral, as well as the best-preserved, best-catalogued

ABOVE: The Monks' Dormitory provides a dramatic entrance to the museum, where visitors can experience the vast size of the only intact surviving monastic dormitory in England

RIGHT: Alexander Pope's translation of Homer's *The Iliad* in the Refectory Library

well as the best-preserved, best-catalogued Benedictine monastic library in the British Isles to survive in its original location. With over 300 manuscripts from the monastic Priory Library still *in situ* on the Durham World Heritage Site, this represents a resource of global significance. Access to Durham Cathedral's manuscript collections and special collections, including the Refectory early printed book, music and antiquary collections, is by appointment only.

CVTHBERTVS

Durham Cathedral's major collection of early printed books, manuscripts and music is housed in the Refectory Library

LEFT: St Cuthbert; monk, bishop, hermit, saint – sculpture by Tim Chalk

The Great Kitchen

The fourteenth-century Great Kitchen is one of only two intact surviving medieval monastic kitchens in England, with a distinctive octagonal shape and high rib-vaulted ceiling. It is now a fitting and permanent home to the most precious and sacred of the cathedral's collections – The Treasures of St Cuthbert. The display cases are environmentally controlled to current British exhibition standards, creating the opportunity to display short-term loans from the collections of other institutions.

The kitchen's scale reflects the size of the community that would have been resident at the cathedral at the time of its construction – up to 100 monks. It would have been a hive of activity, producing a loaf of bread for each monk every day. The monastic diet also included fish, oyster and even porpoise, as evidenced by the archaeological discoveries made during the preparatory restoration work.

After the dissolution of the monasteries between 1536 and 1541, the space continued to be used as a working kitchen until the mid-1940s. Cooking features, including fireplaces, a bread oven and a spit, have been preserved to celebrate its original purpose.

The Treasures of St Cuthbert are the relics associated with this great Anglo-Saxon saint: objects that belonged to and were used by him during his lifetime, together with objects given to his shrine in veneration of his sainthood. The majority of these were removed from his shrine in 1827, one of at least four occasions when it has been opened, since his death in 687.

The coffin is the one made for Cuthbert in 698, 11 years after his death, when his body was discovered to be incorrupt and his sainthood

recognised. Carved images of Christ, the Virgin Mary, apostles and archangels are still visible on the extremely well-preserved fragments, one of the most important surviving pre-Norman Conquest wooden artefacts.

The pectoral cross was probably worn by Cuthbert during his lifetime and buried with him in 687. This gold and garnet jewel, an exquisite piece of Anglo-Saxon metalwork, was discovered in 1827 hidden in his robes, undisturbed for over 1100 years. At the dissolution, Henry VIII's commissioners stripped St Cuthbert's shrine

CLOCKWISE FROM TOP LEFT:
The pectoral cross, the ceiling of the Great Kitchen, St Cuthbert's comb, St Cuthbert's coffin and the Conyers falchion

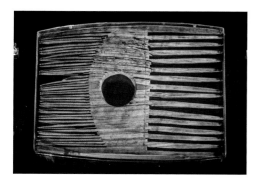

of everything valuable and broke into his tomb, but clearly did not find the cross.

Other objects include the portable altar used by Cuthbert during his lifetime and his ivory comb, which is made from a single piece of ivory with 40 thin teeth on one side and 16 thick teeth on the other. It has been compared with Coptic combs from the fourth to seventh centuries. The early tenth-century stole and maniple were offered in honour of St Cuthbert by King Athelstan in 934, when the Community of St Cuthbert was temporarily settled at Chester-le-Street. They are the only surviving Anglo-Saxon embroideries that depict human figures, again recovered from St Cuthbert's shrine when it was opened in 1827.

The original twelfth-century sanctuary ring is also on display, along with the Conyers falchion. The ring dates from c.1155–60 and reflects the medieval tradition whereby offenders who touched the knocker on the north door of the cathedral would be granted 37 days protection from secular authorities. The ring on the north door today is a replica, made in 1980.

The Conyers falchion is a thirteenth-century medieval sword that once belonged to the Conyers family; only four swords of this type are known to exist in Europe. A medieval Sir John Conyers supposedly used it to slay a giant worm or dragon that was terrorising the village of Sockburn at the time. Lewis Carroll grew up near Sockburn and the story is believed to have inspired his poem 'Jabberwocky'. The tradition is to present the sword to a new bishop of Durham on a bridge over the River Tees when the bishop first enters the diocese. The original was presented to Bishop Paul Butler in February 2014 for the last time; a replica now exists for ceremonial use.

Pilgrimage and Community Galleries

The twelfth-century covey was originally an outdoor kitchen yard, which created a firebreak between the Great Kitchen and the south range of the cloister housing the refectory where the monks gathered to eat. The original wooden serving hatch is still visible as you enter the Pilgrimage Gallery from the Great Kitchen.

The Pilgrimage Gallery is an interactive exhibition space that encourages visitors to become part of the ongoing story of pilgrimage to Durham Cathedral, and to consider their own reasons for visiting the cathedral in the context of pilgrimage both past and present. The intimate space of the Community Gallery is designed to host a rolling programme of spotlight exhibitions featuring work from local community groups and schools. The cathedral offers a diverse learning and outreach programme to engage new audiences with its life and work.

From the Community Gallery, you return to the medieval cloister via the covey. On the way, look out for the eleventh-century staircase uncovered during the museum's restoration work. In the cloister, you may wish to take a well-deserved break in the Undercroft Restaurant, or to browse the Cathedral Shop, before exploring the cathedral, inspired by the stories and fascinating facts you have learnt during your visit to the museum.

Originally, parts of the cloister may have been glassed in; the cloister walkways would have been the hub of the monastery's daily life, linking the principal working buildings. Even today this part of the cathedral conveys a sense of how the activities of the monastery were inseparably connected to one another and to the community's principal purpose, the daily worship of God. Here the monks exercised, taught, studied, copied manuscripts, music and liturgical books and washed: the stone basin in the middle of the grass is what remains of their lavabo. The cloister was laid out when the cathedral was begun, though much of it now dates from the fifteenth century and later.

The south-west door from the cathedral into the cloister is worth admiring from the outside, both for its medieval timber and ironwork, and for the Romanesque decoration of its portal. To the left, or clockwise, in the cloister is another fine example, the Prior's Door. The next entrance leads into the slype, once a simple passage, later the monks' parlour. Next door is the chapter house, where the daily business of the monastery was transacted, the monks sitting on stone benches set into the walls. It was said to be the finest Norman chapter house in England, before its partial demolition in 1796 to create a warmer environment for eighteenth-century clergy. It was rebuilt in the original style in 1895. Today it serves as a vestry, and although not generally open to the public it is occasionally used for public events such as concerts or talks.

From the cloister, a vaulted passage called the Dean's Walk leads into the College. This is the name given in Durham to the cathedral close, another reminder of its monastic past and the 'college' or community of the priory. This peaceful 'village within a city' is the home of the cathedral clergy and others associated with its life, including the chorister school where the cathedral choristers and other children age three to thirteen are educated. The school, founded in 1416, is over 600 years old. The deanery, the building nearest the cloister entrance, has been the home of the priors and deans of Durham since medieval times. The thirteenth-century undercroft below has been transformed into a chapel, with contemporary furniture by Colin Wilbourn. It is dedicated to the Holy Cross and is open to the public during the summer months.

When you have have finished your time at the cathedral itself, you can access the city centre woodlands and riverbanks from the College. The riverbanks are largely owned by the cathedral and provide a wonderful green haven in the middle of the city. They have not always been so green, however, as the Normans stripped them of their vegetation for defensive reasons. In the eighteenth century they were designed and planted as a pleasure garden which forms the basis of their structure today. Prebends' Bridge was built in 1776, to replace an earlier medieval one, and offers spectacular views of the cathedral. Look out for a stone plaque within its north wall with words by Sir Walter Scott.

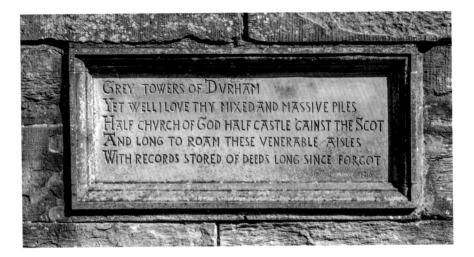

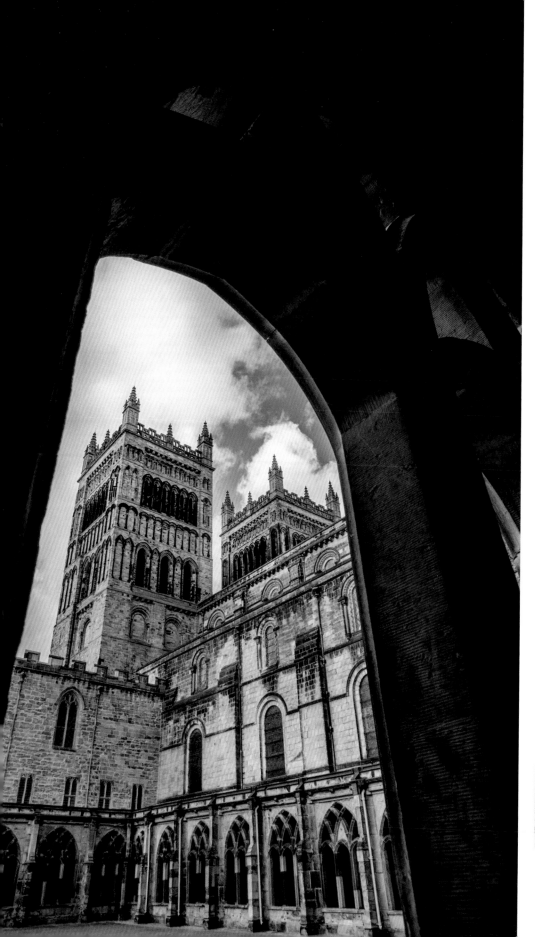

CLOCKWISE FROM FAR LEFT: Stone plaque on Prebends' Bridge; the western towers viewed from the cloister; one of the decorative bosses in the ceiling of the cloister walkway; detail of the medieval metalwork on the south-west door

The cathedral's mission is broad, encompassing many areas of activity: worship and music, outreach and partnership, participation in education, promotion of the arts, stewardship and conservation of this wonderful building, public access to unique collections and artefacts, and a commitment to scholarship and learning. There are many different ways of engagement.

In the widest sense the cathedral belongs to the people of North East England, who have had a deep connection to Durham ever since St Cuthbert's shrine was first set up on this site. Occasions such as the annual Miners' Festival service, the Festival of Remembrance concert and Remembrance Sunday, the great occasions of Christmas and Easter, family activities, the museum, cultural events such as Lumiere (the biennial light festival celebrated across Durham), concerts, talks and much more, bring thousands of people into the cathedral. Many who come have a deep Christian faith, many have no faith, and many are people of other faiths and religions who recognise the cathedral as 'holy'. Durham is a place where all can find inspiration.

The cathedral is governed by its Chapter, a body of lay and ordained people, led by the dean. Through the bishop, the cathedral is the mother church of the diocese of Durham, which stretches between the rivers Tees and Tyne, taking in the course of the river Wear that flows through the heart of Durham and winds around the cathedral. Large diocesan services, such as the ordination of clergy, regularly gather people from all over the diocese. Cathedral clergy share actively in the mission of the diocese by preaching and taking services in parishes. The wider communities of Durham City, University, County and North East England have close relationships with the cathedral and hold regular services and events in the building.

The cathedral's ministry is multi-faceted and takes many forms but at its heart is the rhythm of daily services: Holy Communion and Morning and

Evening Prayer or Evensong. These are offered every day of the year, sometimes with huge congregations and sometimes with a few, always to the glory of God.

Choral Evensong is one of the treasures of cathedral life. There has been a choir of boys and men at Durham for centuries, reaching back to monastic times. The year 2009 saw the introduction of girl choristers, with each set of trebles singing services in turn with the altos, tenors and basses, sharing the demanding workload equally. For special services and events they all sing together.

When the Cathedral Choir is on holiday, visiting choirs are welcomed from North East England, from other parts of the UK and from around the world. They share in the cathedral's ministry and take away wonderful memories of singing in such a special place. On Sundays, a large and lively community of all ages, including children and young people who attend Sunday School, and students resident in Durham, gather for sung Eucharist.

In addition to formal worship the cathedral is a place for personal and private spirituality. People come here daily to sit quietly, light candles, pray or ponder, or find 'sanctuary' by bringing their troubles to the sympathetic ear of trained listeners or volunteer chaplains. A large team of volunteers, alongside staff, welcome upwards of 750,000 guests, visitors and pilgrims every year.

The life of the cathedral reaches beyond worship or prayer. Its education service provides interpretative visits for primary and secondary schoolchildren from across the region. The museum offers a world-class exhibition experience, takes visitors on a journey through the most intact medieval monastic buildings, refashioned as exhibition spaces offering both permanent displays and an innovative rolling exhibition programme, enabling visitors to discover the story of Christianity in North East England through interpretation and the display of artefacts.

The library, with its incomparable collection of books and manuscripts, is a working environment

that serves the needs of both students of theology and those engaged in specialised research. Partnerships, such as serving as a drop-off point for contributions to Durham food bank and gifts for children at Christmas, help to support disadvantaged communities. There is a flourishing programme of concerts and arts events and a highly successful music outreach programme, enabling children in the region's state schools to sing with the choristers, with further opportunities to join one of the cathedral's voluntary choirs. The cathedral's own chorister school educates up to 200 children from kindergarten to age 13, offering the benefits of independent education in the cathedral's precincts.

The cathedral also has active working relationships with other independent and maintained schools in the City and County, with Durham University, Durham County Council, local prisons, and with the retail, commercial and charitable sectors within the region. Study programmes promote the understanding of the Christian faith through reading groups, theological lectures and opportunities to explore Durham's Anglo-Saxon and Benedictine heritage. In this the cathedral benefits from its proximity to the university and its renowned Department of Theology and Religion. The museum is enhancing the cathedral's social and economic contribution to the wider community of North East England through employment, partnership and outreach. The cathedral building itself plays a key role as Durham City and County seek to maximise tourism and visitors to the city and region.

Caring for the building is a huge part of the cathedral's mission, conserving it as a living place for generations to come; there are always challenges, both financial and practical. The staff team includes talented stonemasons, joiners, electricians and gardeners, supplemented by external contractors when appropriate. They keep the building in working order, although at times the task in hand can seem enormous.

Like all cathedrals, Durham is shaped by its history, by the challenges of the day and by the vision and aspiration of the people who care for and serve it. It is cherished equally by those who live, work and study in the region as by those who come to visit. We hope that you find it a place of prayer, inspiration and peace.

Like all cathedrals, Durham is shaped by its history, by the challenges of the day and by the vision and aspiration of the people who care for and serve it